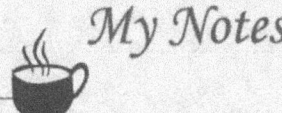 

My Notes

 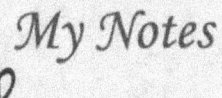

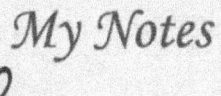 

My Notes

 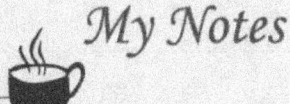

My Notes

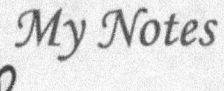 

My Notes

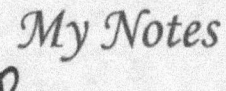 

My Notes

Coffee Tasting Journal

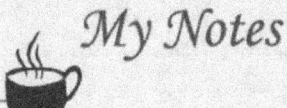 

My Notes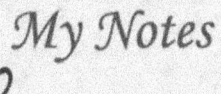

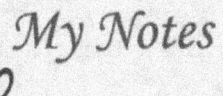 

My Notes

All I want to do is drink coffee all day long

 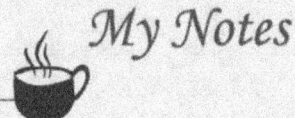

 **My Notes**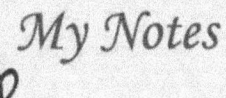

 # My Notes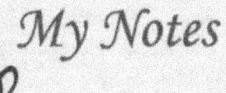

 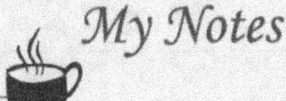

 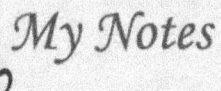

 My Notes

 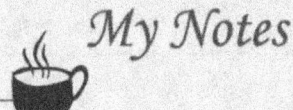

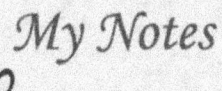 

My Notes

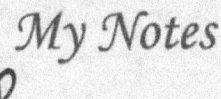 

My Notes

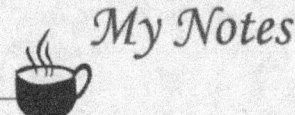 

My Notes

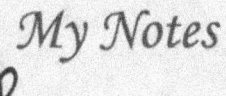 

All I want to do is drink coffee all day long

Coffee Tasting Journal

 **My Notes**

My Notes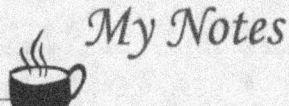

All I want to do is drink coffee all day long

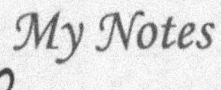 

My Notes

 # My Notes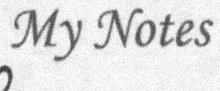

 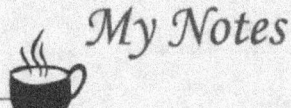

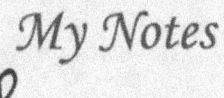 

My Notes

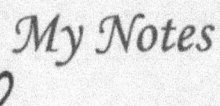 

My Notes

Coffee Tasting Journal

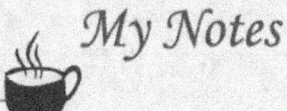 

My Notes

 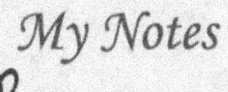

 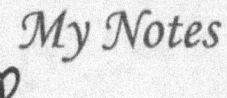

My Notes

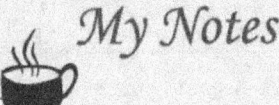 My Notes

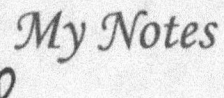 

My Notes

 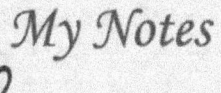

Coffee Tasting Journal

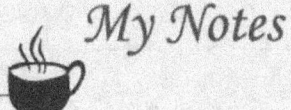 

My Notes

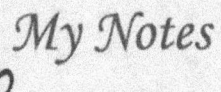 

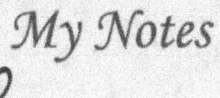 

My Notes

All I want to do is drink coffee all day long

 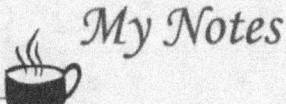

My Notes

 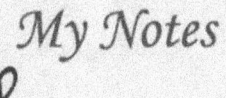 My Notes

My Notes

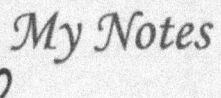 

All I want to do is drink coffee all day long

 # 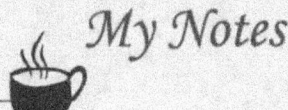 My Notes

 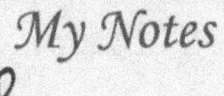

My Notes

All I want to do is drink coffee all day long

 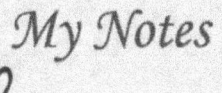

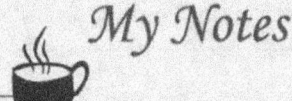 **My Notes**

Coffee Tasting Journal

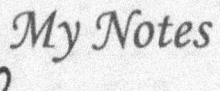 **My Notes**

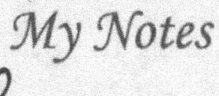 

My Notes

 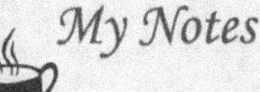

My Notes

 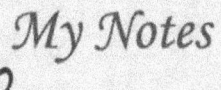

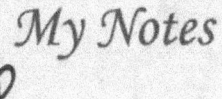 **My Notes**

All I want to do is drink coffee all day long

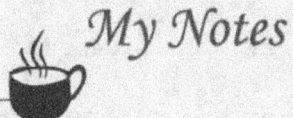 

My Notes

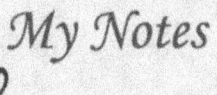 

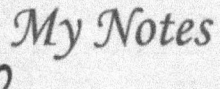 

My Notes

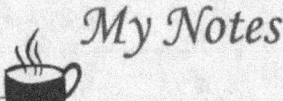 My Notes

All I want to do is drink coffee all day long

 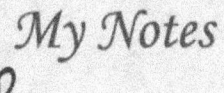 My Notes

Coffee Tasting Journal

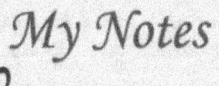 

All I want to do is drink coffee all day long

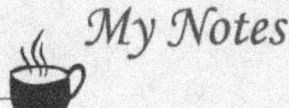 

Coffee Tasting Journal

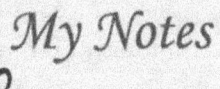 

My Notes

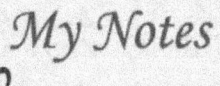 

My Notes

 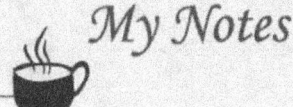

 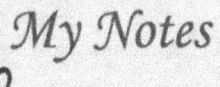

All I want to do is drink coffee all day long

 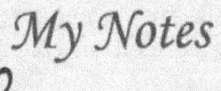

My Notes

Coffee Tasting Journal

www.ingramcontent.com/pod-product-compliance
Lightning Source LLC
LaVergne TN
LVHW012116070526
838202LV00056B/5745